The Heart of the New Thought by Ella Wheeler Wilcox

Born on November 5th 1850 in Johnstown, Wisconsin, Ella Wheeler was the youngest of four children. She began to write as a child and by the time she graduated was already well known as a poet throughout Wisconsin.

Regarded more as a popular poet than a literary poet her most famous work 'Solitude' reflects on a train journey she made where giving comfort to a distressed fellow traveller she wrote how the others grief imposed itself for a time on her 'Laugh and the world laughs with you, Weep and you weep alone'. It was published in 1883 and was immensely popular.

The following year, 1884, she married Robert Wilcox. They lived for a time in New York before moving to Connecticut. Their only child, a son, died shortly after birth. It was around this time they developed an interest in spiritualism which for Ella would develop further into an interest in the occult. In later years this and works on positive thinking would occupy much of her writing.

On Robert's death in 1916 she spent months waiting for word from him from 'the other side' which never came.

In this volume she gives her views on New Thought. It is an interesting diversion from her poetry and helps us to more readily understand some of the influences that made her such a popular figure on the poetical scene.

In 1918 she published her autobiography The Worlds And I.

Ella died of cancer on October 30th, 1919.

Publishers' Preface

This book is noteworthy as an interpretation of "New Thought."

That which was vague, mystic, unreal, has become, in the hands of Mrs. Wilcox, a lovable philosophy of simplest construction.

The backbone of this philosophy is The Power of Right Thought.

Startling as are some of the tenets expressed, they are provably true here and now.

It is possible that the very simplicity of this book will encourage careless criticism from those who believe that genius and ambiguity are twin.

But Mrs. Wilcox is ever the voice of the people: what she says is practical; what she thinks is clear; what she feels is plain.

Let the people judge this book.

Index Of Contents
Let the Past Go
The Sowing of the Seed
Old Clothes
High Noon
Obstacles
Thought Force
Opulence
Eternity
Morning Influences
The Philosophy of Happiness
A Worn Out Creed
Common Sense
Literature
Optimism
Preparation
Dividends
Royalty
Heredity
Invincibility
Faces
The Object of Life
Wisdom
Self-Conquest
The Important Trifles
Concentration
Destiny
Sympathy
The Breath
Generosity
Woman's Opportunity
Balance
Ella Wheeler Wilcox – A Short Biography
Ella Wheeler Wilcox – A Concise Bibliography

THE HEART OF THE NEW THOUGHT

Let the Past Go

Do not begin the new year by recounting to yourself or others all your losses and sorrows.

Let the past go.

Should some good friend present you with material for a lovely garment, would you insult her by throwing it aside and describing the beautiful garments you had worn out in past times?

The new year has given you the fabric for a fresh start in life, why dwell upon the events which have gone, the joys, blessings and advantages of the past!

Do not tell me it is too late to be successful or happy. Do not tell me you are sick or broken in spirit, the spirit cannot be sick or broken, because it is of God.

It is your mind which makes your body sick. Let the spirit assert itself and demand health and hope and happiness in this new year.

Forget the money you have lost, the mistakes you have made, the injuries you have received, the disappointments you have experienced.

Real sorrow, the sorrow which comes from the death of dear ones, or some great cross well borne, you need not forget. But think of these things as sent to enrich your nature, and to make you more human and sympathetic. You are missing them if you permit yourself instead to grow melancholy and irritable.

It is weak and unreasonable to imagine destiny has selected you for special suffering.

Sorrow is no respecter of persons. Say to yourself with the beginning of this year that you are going to consider all your troubles as an education for your mind and soul; and that out of the experiences which you have passed through you are going to build a noble and splendid character, and a successful career.

Do not tell me you are too old.

Age is all imagination. Ignore years and they will ignore you.

Eat moderately, and bathe freely in water as cold as nature's rainfall. Exercise thoroughly and regularly.

Be alive, from crown to toe. Breathe deeply, filling every cell of the lungs for at least five minutes, morning and night, and when you draw in long, full breaths, believe you are inhaling health, wisdom and success.

Anticipate good health. If it does not come at once, consider it a mere temporary delay, and continue to expect it.

Regard any physical ailment as a passing inconvenience, no more.

Never for an instant believe you are permanently ill or disabled.

The young men of France are studying alchemy, hoping to learn the secret of the transmutation of gold.

If you will study your own spirit and its limitless powers, you will gain a greater secret than any alchemist ever held; a secret which shall give you whatever you desire.

Think of your body as the silver jewel box, your mind as the silk lining, your spirit as the gem. Keep the box burnished and clear of dust, but remember always that the jewel within is the precious part of it.

Think of yourself as on the threshold of unparalleled success. A whole, clear, glorious year lies before you! In a year you can regain health, fortune, restfulness, happiness!

Push on! Achieve, achieve!

The Sowing of the Seed

When you start in the "New Thought" do not expect sudden illumination. Do not imagine that you are to become perfectly well, perfectly cheerful, successful, and a healer, in a few days.

Remember all growth is slow.

Mushrooms spring up in a night, but oaks grow with deliberation and endure for centuries.

Mental and spiritual power must be gained by degrees.

If you attained maturity before you entered this field of "New Thought" it is folly to suppose a complete transformation of your whole being will take place in a week, a month, or a year.

All you can reasonably look for is a gradual improvement, just as you might do if you were attempting to take up music or a science.

The New Thought is a science, the Science of Right Thinking. But the brain cells which have been shaped by the old thoughts of despondency and fear, cannot all at once be reformed.

It will be a case of "Try, try again."

Make your daily assertions, "I am love, health, wisdom, cheerfulness, power for good, prosperity, success, usefulness, opulence."

Never fail to assert these things at least twice a day; twenty times is better. But if you do not attain to all immediately, if your life does not at once exemplify your words, let it not discourage you.

The saying of the words is the watering of the seeds.

After a time they will begin to sprout, after a longer time to cover the barren earth with grain, after a still longer time to yield a harvest.

If you have been accustomed to feeling prejudices and dislikes easily, you will not all at once find it easy to illustrate your assertion, "I am love." If you have indulged yourself in thoughts of disease, the old aches and pains will intrude even while you say "I am health!"

If you have groveled in fear and a belief that you were born to poverty and failure, courage and success and opulence will be of slow growth. Yet they will grow and materialize, as surely as you insist and persist.

Declare they are yours, right in the face of the worst disasters. There is nothing so confuses and flustrates misfortune as to stare it down with hopeful unflinching eyes.

If you waken some morning in the depths of despondency and gloom, do not say to yourself:

"I may as well give up this effort to adopt the New Thought, I have made a failure of it evidently." Instead sit down quietly, and assert calmly that you are cheerfulness, hope, courage, faith and success.

Realize that your despondency is only temporary; an old habit, which is reasserting itself, but over which you will gradually gain the ascendency. Then go forth into the world and busy yourself in some useful occupation, and before you know it is on the way, hope will creep into your heart, and the gray cloud will lift from your mind. Physical pains will loosen their hold, and conditions of poverty will change to prosperity.

Your mind is your own to educate and direct.

You can do it by the aid of the Spirit, but you must be satisfied to work slowly.

Be patient and persistent.

Old Clothes

As you go over your wardrobe in the spring or fall, do not keep any old, useless, or even questionable, garments, for "fear you might need them another year."

Give them to the ragman, or send them to the county or city poor house. There is nothing that will keep you in a rut of shabbiness more than clinging to old clothes.

It is useless to say that you cannot afford new garments.

It is because you have harped upon this idea that you are still in straitened circumstances.

You believe neither in God or yourself.

Possibly you were brought up to think yourself a mere worm of earth, born to poverty and sorrow.

If you were, it will of course require a continued effort to train your mind to the new thought, the thought of your divine inheritance of all God's vast universe of wealth.

But you can do it.

Begin by giving away your old clothes. There may be people, poor relations, or some struggling mother of half-clad children, to whom your old garments will seem like new raiment, and to whom they will bring hope and happiness.

As a rule, it is not well to give people your discarded clothing.

It has a tendency to lower their self-respect and to make them look to you, instead of to themselves, for support.

It all depends upon whom the people are and how you do it.

If you can find employment for them, and arouse their hope and self-confidence and ambition, it is better than carloads of clothing or furniture or provisions.

But little children, suffering from cold, or hard-working, over-taxed men and women, will not be harmed, and may be temporarily cheered and encouraged by your gifts.

No matter if you still need your frayed-out garments, do not keep them.

Your thoughts of poverty and trouble have impregnated them so that you will continue to produce the same despondent mind stuff while you wear these garments.

Get rid of them, and believe that you are to soon procure fresh, becoming raiment.

Rouse all your energies, and go straight ahead with that purpose in mind.

You will be surprised to find how soon the opportunity presents itself for you to obtain what you need.

There is new strength, repose of mind and inspiration in fresh apparel.

God gives Nature new garments every season. We are a part of Nature.

He gives us the qualities and the opportunities to obtain suitable covering for our changing needs, if we believe in the one, and use the other.

When I read of a wealthy man who boasts that he has worn one hat seven years, or a woman in affluent circumstances who has worn one bonnet for various seasons, I feel sorry for their ignorance and ashamed of their penuriousness.

Look at the apple-tree, with its delicate spring drapery, its luxurious summer foliage, its autumn richness of coloring, its winter draperies of white! Surely the Creator did not intend the tree to have more variety than man!

The tree trusts, and grows, and takes storm and sun as divinely sent, and believes in its right to new apparel, and it comes.

It will come to you if you do the same.

High Noon

Every woman who passes thirty ought to keep her brain, heart and mind alive and warm with human sympathy and emotion. She ought to interest herself in the lives of others, and make her friendship valuable to the young.

She should keep her body supple, and avoid losing the lines of grace: and she should select some study or work to occupy her spare hours and to lend a zest to the coming years. Every woman in the comfortable walks in life can find time for such a study. No woman of tact, charm, refinement and feeling need ever let her husband, unless she has married a clod, become indifferent or commonplace in his treatment of her. Man reflects to an astonishing degree woman's sentiments for him.

Keep sentiment alive in your own heart, madam, and in the heart of your husband. If he sees that other men admire you he will be more alert to the necessity of remaining your lover.

Take the happy, safe, medium path between a gray and a gay life by keeping it radiant and bright. Read and think and talk of cheerful, hopeful, interesting subjects. Avoid small gossip, and be careful in your criticism of neighbors. Sometimes we must criticise, but speak to people whose faults you feel a word of counsel may amend, not of them to others.

Make your life after it reaches its noon, glorious with sunlight, rich with harvests, and bright with color. Be alive in mind, heart and body. Be joyous without giddiness, loving without silliness, attractive without being flirtatious, attentive to others' needs without being officious, and instructive without too great a display of erudition.

Be a noble, loving, lovable woman.

It is never too late in life to make anew start. No matter how small a beginning may be, it is so much begun for a new incarnation if it is cut off here by death.

If I were one hundred years old, and in possession of my faculties, I would not hesitate to undertake a new enterprise which offered a hope of bettering my condition.

Thought is eternal in its effects, and every hopeful thought which enters the mind sets vibrations in motion, which shall help minds millions of miles distant and lives yet unborn.

It is folly to mourn over a failure to provide opportunities and luxuries for children. We have only to look at the children of the rich, to see how little enduring happiness money gives, and how seldom great advantages result in great characters. The majority of the really great people of the world, in all lines of achievement, have sprung from poverty. I do not mean from pauper homes, but from the homes where only the mere necessities of life could be obtained, and where early in their youth the children felt it necessary to go into the world and make their own way. Self-dependence, self-reliance, energy, ambition, were all developed in this way.

How rarely do we find these qualities in the children of wealth. How rarely do great philosophers, great statesman, great thinkers and great characters develop from the wealthy classes.

Pauperism, infant labor, the wage-earning women, are all evils which ought to be abolished. But next to that evil I believe the worst thing possible for a human soul is to be born to wealth. It is an obstacle to greatness which few are strong enough to surmount, and it rarely results in happiness to the recipient.

Obstacles

However great the obstacles between you and your goal may be or have been, do not lay the blame of your failure upon them.

Other people have succeeded in overcoming just as great obstacles.

Remove such hindrances from the path for others, if you can, or tell them a way to go around. Even lead them a little distance and cheer them on.

But so far as you yourself are concerned, do not stop to excuse any delinquency or half-heartedness or defeat by the plea of circumstance or environment.

The great nature makes its own environment, and dominates circumstance.

It all depends upon the amount of force in your own soul.

While you apply this rule to yourself and make no scapegoat of "fate," you must have consideration for the weakness of others, and you must try and better the conditions of the world as you go along.

You are robust and possessed of all your limbs. You can mount over the great boulder which has fallen in the road to success, and go on your way to your goal all the stronger for the experience.

But behind you comes a one-legged man, a blind man, a man bowed to the earth with a heavy burden, which he cannot lay down.

It will require weeks, months, years of effort on their part to climb over that rock which you surmounted in a few hours.

So it is right and just for you to call other strong ones to your aid and roll the boulder away or blast it out of the path.

That is just exactly the way you should think of the present industrial conditions.

In spite of them, the strong, well-poised, earnest and determined soul can reach any desired success.

But there are boulders in the road which do not belong there, boulders which cause hundreds of the pilgrims who are lame or blind or burdened, to fall by the wayside and perish.

It is your duty to aid in removing these obstacles and in making the road a safe and clear thoroughfare for all who journey.

Do not sit down by the roadside and say you have been hindered by these difficulties, that is to confess yourself weak.

Do not mount over them and rush to your goal and say coldly to the throngs behind you, "Oh, everybody can climb over that rock who really tries, didn't I?" That is to announce yourself selfish and unsympathetic.

No doubt the lame, the blind and the burdened could attain the goal despite the rocks if they were fired by a consciousness of the divine force within them; that consciousness can achieve all things under all circumstances.

But there will always be thousands of pilgrims toiling wearily toward the goal who have not come to this realization.

If there are unjust, unfair and unkind restrictions placed about them, see to it that you do all in your power to right what is wrong.

But never wait to attain your own success because of these restrictions or obstacles.

Believe absolutely in your own God-given power to overcome anything and everything.

Think of yourself as performing miracles with God's aid.

Desire success so intensely that you attract if as the magnet attracts the steel

Help to adjust things as you go along, but never for a moment believe that the lack of adjustment can cause you to fail.

Thought Force

Your spirit and mine are both part of the stupendous cause. We have always been, and always will be. First in one form, then in another.

Every thought, word and deed is helping decide your next place in the Creator's magnificent universe. You will be beautiful or ugly, wise or ignorant, fortunate or unfortunate, according to what use you make of yourself here and now.

Unselfish thoughts, training your mind to desire only universal good, the cultivation of the highest attributes, such as love, honesty, gratitude, faith, reverence and good will, all mean a life of usefulness and happiness in another incarnation, as well as satisfaction and self-respect in this sphere.

Even if you escape the immediate results of the opposite course of action here, you must face the law of cause and effect in the next state. It is inevitable. God, the maker of all things, does not change His laws. "As you sow you reap." "As a man thinketh so is he." There is no "revenge" in God's mind. He simply makes His laws, and we work our destinies for good or ill according to our adherence to them or violation of them.

Each one of us is a needed part of His great plan. Let each soul say: "He has need of me or I would not be. I am here to strengthen the plan." Remember that always in your most discouraged hours.

The Creator makes no mistakes.

There is a divine purpose in your being on earth. Think of yourself as necessary to the great design. It is an inspiring thought. And then consider the immensity of the universe and how accurately the Maker planned it all.

Do not associate with pessimists. If you are unfortunate enough to be the son or daughter, husband or wife of one, put cotton (either real or spiritual) in your ears, and shut out the poison words of discouragement and despondency.

No tie of blood or law should compel you to listen to what means discomfort and disaster to you.

Get out and away, into the society of optimistic people.

Before you go, insist on saying cheerful, hopeful and bright things, sowing the seed, as it were, in the mental ground behind you. But do not sit down to see it grow.

Never feel that it is your duty to stay closely and continuously in the atmosphere of the despondent.

You might as well think it your duty to stay in deep water with one who would not make the least effort to swim.

Get on shore and throw out a life-line, but do not remain and be dragged under.

If you find any one determined to talk failure and sickness and misfortune and disaster, walk away.

You would not permit the dearest person on earth to administer slow poison to you if you knew it. Then why think it your duty to take mental potions which paralyze your courage and kill your ambition?

Despondency is one phase of immorality. It is blasphemous and an insult to the Creator.

You are justified in avoiding the people who send you from their presence with less hope and force and strength to cope with life's problems than when you met them.

Do what you can to change their current of thought. But do not associate intimately with them until they have learned to keep silent, at least, if they cannot speak hopefully.

Learn how to walk, how to poise your body, how to breathe, how to hold your head, how to focus your mind on things of universal importance. Believe your tender, loving thoughts and wishes for good to all humanity have power to help the struggling souls of earth to rise to higher and better conditions. No matter how limited your sphere of action may seem to you and how small your town appears on the map, if you develop your mental and spiritual forces through love thoughts you can be a power to move the world along. Rise up and realize your strength. Not only will you be more useful and happy, but you will grow more beautiful and keep your youth.

Opulence

Do not go through the world talking poverty and asking everyone you deal with to show you special consideration because you are "poor" and "unfortunate."

If you do this with an idea of saving a few dollars here and there, you will always have to do it, because you are creating poverty conditions by your constant assertions.

It is a curious fact that the people who are always demanding consideration in money matters demand the best that is going at the same time.

I have known a woman to make a plea for cut prices in a boarding house because she was so poor, yet she wanted the sunniest room and the best location the house afforded.

It is the charity patients who make the most complaint of a physician's skill or a nurse's attention.

If you cannot afford to do certain things, or buy certain objects, don't. But when you decide you must, decide, too, that you will pay the price, and make no whining plea of poverty.

There are two extremes of people in the world, one as distasteful as the other. One is represented by the man who boasts of the costliness of every possession, and invites the whole world to behold his opulence and expenditure.

His clothes, his house, his servants, his habits, seem no different to the observer from his neighbor's, yet, according to his story, they cost ten times the amount.

The other extreme is the man who dresses well, lives well, enjoys all the comforts and pleasures of his associates, yet talks poverty continually, and expects the entire community to show him consideration in consequence.

Another thing to avoid is the role of the chronically injured person.

We all know him.

He has a continual grievance. He has been cheated, abused, wronged, insulted, disappointed and deceived. We wonder how or why he has managed to exist, as we listen to the story of his troubles.

No one ever treats him fairly, either in business or social life. Everybody is ungrateful, unkind, selfish, and he could not be made to believe that these experiences were of his own making.

All of us meet with occasional blows from fate, in the form of insults, or ingratitude, or trickery from an unexpected source.

But if we get nothing else but those disappointing experiences from life, we may rest assured the fault lies somewhere in ourselves.

We are not sending out the right kind of mental stuff, or we would get better returns.

You never can tell what your thoughts will do
In bringing you hate or love,
For thoughts are things, and their airy wings
Are swift as a carrier dove.
They follow the law of the universe
Each thing must create its kind,
And they speed o'er the track to bring you back
Whatever went out from your mind.

In the main, we must of necessity get from humanity what we give to it. If we question our ability to win friends or love, people will also question it.

If we doubt our own judgment and discretion in business, others will doubt it, and the shrewd and unprincipled will take the opportunity given by our doubts of ourselves, to spring upon us.

If in consequence we distrust every person we meet, we create an unwholesome and unfortunate atmosphere about ourselves, which will bring to us the unworthy and deceitful. Stand firm in the universe. Believe in yourself. Believe in others.

If you make a mistake, consider it only an incident.

If someone wrongs you, cheats, misuses or insults you, let it pass as one of the lessons you had to learn, but do not imagine that you are selected by fate for only such lessons. Keep wholesome, hopeful and sympathetic with the world at large, whatever individuals may do. Expect life to use you better every year, and it will not disappoint you in the long run. For life is what we make it.

Eternity

Do you know what a wonderfully complicated thing a human being is? Every feature, every portion of your body, every motion you make, reflects your mental organization.

I know a woman past middle life who has always been on the opposite side of every question discussed in her presence.

She was agnostic with the orthodox, reverential with atheists, liberal with the narrow, bigoted with the liberal.

Whatever belief any one expressed on any subject, she invariably took the other extreme. She loved to disagree with her fellow-men. It was her pastime.

Now, to walk with that woman in silence is merely to carry on a wordless argument.

You cannot regulate your steps so they will harmonize with hers. She will be just ahead or just behind you, and if you want to turn to the left, she pulls to the right. A promenade with her is more exhausting than a day's labor.

She is not conscious of it, and would think anyone very unreasonable and unjust who told her of her peculiarities.

I know a woman who all her life has been looking afar for happiness and peace and content, and has never found any of them, because she did not look in her own soul.

She was a restless girl, and she married, believing in domestic life lay the goal of her dreams. But she was not happy there, and sighed for freedom. She wanted to move, and did move, once, twice, thrice, to different points of the United States. She was discontented with each change. She is to-day possessed of all comforts and luxuries which life can afford, yet she is the same restless soul. She likes to read, but it is always the book which she does not possess which she craves. If she is in the library with shelves book-filled, she goes into the garret and hunts in old boxes for a book or a paper which has been cast aside.

If she is in a picture gallery, she wants to go to the window and look out on the street, but when she is on the street it bores her, and she longs to go in the house.

If a member of the family is absent, she gets no enjoyment out of the society of those at home; yet when that absent one returns her mind strays elsewhere, seeking some imagined happiness not found here.

I wonder if such souls ever find it, even in the spirit realm, or if they go on there seeking and always seeking something just beyond. It is a great gift to learn to enjoy the present, to get all there is out of it, and to think of to-day as a piece of eternity. Begin now to teach yourself this great art if you have not thought of it before. To be able to enjoy heaven, one must learn first to enjoy earth.

Morning Influences

What do you think about the very first thing in the morning?

Your thoughts during the first half-hour of the morning will greatly influence the entire day. You may not realize this, but it is nevertheless a fact.

If you set out with worry, and depression, and bitterness of soul toward fate or man, you are giving the key note to a day of discords and misfortunes.

If you think peace, hope and happiness, you are sounding a note of harmony and success.

The result may not be felt at once, but it will not fail to make itself evident eventually.

Control your morning thoughts. You can do it.

The first moment on waking, no matter what your mood, say to yourself: "I will get all the comfort and pleasure possible out of this day, and I will do something to add to the measure of the world's happiness or well-being. I will control myself when tempted to be irritable or unhappy, I will look for the bright side of every event."

Once you say these things over to yourself in a calm, earnest way, you will begin to feel more cheerful. The worries and troubles of the coming day will seem less colossal.

Then say: "I shall be given help to meet anything that comes to-day. Everything will be for the best. I shall succeed in whatever I undertake. I cannot fail."

Do not let it discourage you if the moment you leave your room you encounter a trouble or a disaster. This usually happens. When we make any boasts, spiritually or physically, we are put to the test. The occult forces about us are not unlike human beings. When a school-boy boasts of his strength, and says he can "lick any boy in school," he generally gets a chance to prove it.

When we declare we are brave enough to overcome any fate, we find our strength put to the test at once.

But that is all right. Prove your words to be true. Regard the troubles and cares you encounter as the "punching bags" of fate, given you to develop your spiritual muscle.

Go at them with courage and keep to your morning resolve.

By and by the troubles will lessen, and you will find yourself master of Circumstances.

The Philosophy of Happiness

There are natures born to happiness just as there are born musicians, mechanics and mathematicians.

They are usually children who came into life under right pre-natal conditions. That is, children conceived and born in love.

The mother who thanks God for the little life she is about to bring to earth, gives her child a more blessed endowment than if it were heir to a kingdom or a fortune.

As the majority of people, however, born under "civilized" conditions, are unwelcome to their mothers, it is rarely we encounter one who has a birthright of happiness.

Youth possesses a certain buoyancy and exhilaration which passes for happiness, until the real disposition of the individual asserts itself with the passing of time.

Good health and strong vitality are great aids to happiness; yet that they, wealth and honors added, do not produce that much desired state of mind we have but to look about us to observe.

One who is not born a musician needs to toil more assiduously to acquire skill in the art, however strong his desire or great his taste, than the natural genius.

So the man not endowed with joyous impulses needs to set himself the task of acquiring the habit of happiness. I believe it can be done. To the sad or restless or discontented being I would say: Begin each morning by resolving to find something in the day to enjoy. Look in each experience which comes to you for some grain of happiness. You will be surprised to find how much that has seemed hopelessly disagreeable possesses either an instructive or an amusing side.

There is a certain happiness to be found in the most disagreeable duty when you stop to realize that you are getting it out of the way.

If it is one of those duties which has the uncomfortable habit of repeating itself continually, you can at least say you are learning patience and perseverance, which are two great virtues and essential to any permanent happiness in life.

Do not anticipate the happiness of to-morrow, but discover it in to-day. Unless you are in the profound depths of some great sorrow, you will find it if you look for it.

Think of yourself each morning as an explorer in a new realm. I know a man whose time is gold, and he carefully arranged his plans to take three hours for a certain pleasure. He lost his way and missed his pleasure, but was full of exuberant delight over his "new experience."

"I saw places and met with adventures I might have missed my whole life." He was a true philosopher and optimist and such a man gets the very kernel out of the nut of life.

I know a woman who had since her birth every material blessing, health, wealth, position, travel and a luxurious home. She was forever complaining of the cares and responsibilities of the latter. Finally she prevailed upon the family to rent the home for a series of years and to live in hotels. Now she goes about posing as a martyr, "a homeless woman." It is impossible for such a selfishly perverted nature to know happiness.

A child should be taught from its earliest life to find entertainment in every kind of condition or weather. If it hears its elders cursing and bemoaning a rainy day the child's plastic mind is quick to receive the impression that a rainy day is a disaster.

How much better to expatiate in its presence on the blessing of rain, and to teach it the enjoyment of all nature's varying moods, which other young animals feel.

Happiness must come from within in order to respond to that which comes from without, just as there must be a musical ear and temperament to enjoy music.

Cultivate happiness as an art or science.

A Worn Out Creed

I have a letter from an "orthodox Christian," who says the only hope for humanity lies in the "old-fashioned religion."

Then he proceeds to tell me how carefully he has studied human nature, "in business, in social life, and in himself," and that he finds it all vile, selfish, sinful.

Of course he does, because he studies it from a false and harmful standpoint, and looks for "the worm of earth" and "the poor, miserable sinner," instead of the _divine_ man.

We find what we look for in this world.

I have always been looking for the noble qualities in human beings, and I have found them.

There are great souls all along the highway of life, and there are great qualities even in the people who seem common and weak to us ordinarily.

One of the grandest souls I know is a man who served his term in prison for sins committed while in drink.

He was not "born bad", he simply drifted into bad company and formed bad habits.

He paid the awful penalty of five years behind prison bars, but the divine man within him asserted itself, and today I have no friend I feel prouder to call that name.

Mr. John L. Tait, secretary of the Central Howard Association, of Chicago, writes me regarding his knowledge of ex-convicts:

According to my experience with a number of men of this class during the last two years, more than 90 per cent of them are worthy of the most cordial support and assistance.

If this can be said of men who have been criminals, surely humanity is not so vile as my "orthodox" correspondent would have me believe.

A "Christian" of that order ought to be put under restraint, and not allowed to associate with mankind.

He carries a moral malaria with him, which poisons the air.

He suggests evil to minds which have not thought it.

He is a dangerous hypnotist, while pretending to be a disciple of Christ.

The man who believes that all men are vicious, selfish and immoral is projecting pernicious mind stuff into space, which is as dangerous to the peace of the community as dynamite bombs.

The world has been kept back too long by this false, unholy and blasphemous "religion."

It is not the religion of Christ, it is the religion of ignorant translators, ignorant readers.

Thank God, its supremacy is past. A wholesome and holy religion has taken its place with the intelligent progressive minds of the day, a religion which says: "I am all goodness, love, truth, mercy, health. I am a necessary part of God's universe. I am a divine soul, and only good can come through me or to me. God made me, and He could make nothing but goodness and purity and worth. I am the reflection of all His qualities."

This is the "new" religion; yet it is older than the universe. It is God's own thought put into practical form.

Common Sense

If you are suffering from physical ills, ask yourself if it is not your own fault.

There is scarcely one person in one hundred who does not over eat or drink.

I know an entire family who complain of gastric troubles, yet who keep the coffee pot continually on the range and drink large quantities of that beverage at least twice a day.

No one can be well who does that. Almost every human ailment can be traced to foolish diet.

Eat only two meals in twenty-four hours. If you are not engaged in active physical labor, make it one meal. Drink two or three or four quarts of milk at intervals during the day to supply good blood to the system.

You will thrive upon it, and you will not miss the other two meals after the first week.

And your ailments will gradually disappear.

Meantime, if you are self-supporting, your bank account will increase.

Think of the waste of money which goes into indigestible food! It is appalling when you consider it. Heaven speed the time when men and women find out how little money it requires to sustain the body in good health and keep the brain clear and the eye bright!

The heavy drinker is to-day looked upon with pity and scorn. The time will come when the heavy eater will be similarly regarded.

Once find the delight of a simple diet, the benefit to body and mind and purse, and life will assume new interest, and toil will be robbed of its drudgery, for it will cease to be a mere matter of toiling for a bare existence.

Again, are you unhappy? Stop and ask yourself why. If you have a great sorrow, time will be your consoler. And there is an ennobling and enriching effect of sorrow well borne.

It is the education of the soul. But if you are unhappy over petty worries and trials, you are wearing yourself to no avail; and if you are allowing small things to irritate and harass you and to spoil the beautiful days for you, take yourself in hand and change your ways.

You can do it if you choose. It is pitiful to observe what sort of troubles most unhappy people are afflicted with. I have seen a beautiful young woman grow care lined and faded just from imagining she was being "slighted" or neglected by her acquaintances.

Someone nodded coldly to her, another one spoke superciliously, a third failed to invite her, a fourth did not pay her a call, and so on, always a grievance to relate until one is prepared to look sympathetic at sight of her.

And such petty, petty grievances for this great, good life to be marred by!

And all the result of her own disposition. Had she chosen to look for appreciation and attention and good will she would have found it everywhere.

Then, about your temper? Is it flying loose over a trifle? Are you making yourself and everyone else wretched if a chair is out of place, or a meal a moment late, or some member of the family is tardy at dinner, or your shoe string is in a tangle or your collar button mislaid?

Do you go to pieces nervously if you are obliged to repeat a remark to someone who did not understand you? I have known a home to be ruined by just such infinitesimal annoyances. It is a habit, like the drug or alcohol habit, this irritability.

All you need do is to stop it. Keep your voice from rising, and speak slowly and calmly when you feel yourself giving way to it. Realize how ridiculous and disagreeable you will be if you continue, what an unlovely and hideous old age you are preparing for yourself. And realize that a loose temper is a sign of vulgarity and lack of culture.

Think of the value of each day of life, how much it means and what possibilities of happiness and usefulness it contains if well spent.

But if you stuff yourself like an anaconda, dwell on the small worries and grow angry at the least trifle, you are committing as great and inexcusable a folly as if you flung your furniture and garments and food and fuel into the sea in a spirit of wanton cruelty. You are wasting life for nothing. Every sick, gloomy day you pass is a sin against life. Get health, be cheerful, keep calm.

Clear your mind of every gloomy, selfish angry or revengeful thought. Allow no resentment or grudge toward man or fate to stay in your heart over night.

Wake in the morning with a blessing for every living thing on your lips and in your soul. Say to yourself: "Health, luck, usefulness, success, are mine. I claim them." Keep thinking that thought, no matter what happens, just as you would put one foot before another if you had a mountain to climb. Keep on, keep on, and suddenly you will find you are on the heights, luck beside you.

Whoever follows this recipe cannot fail of happiness, good fortune and a useful life. But saying the words over once and then drifting back to anger, selfishness, revenge and gloom will do no good.

The words must be said over and over, and thought and lived when not said.

Literature

The world is full of "New Thought" Literature. It is helpful and inspiring to read.

It is worth many dollars to anyone who will live its philosophy.

I talked to a man who has been studying along these lines for some years.

"Oh, I know all that philosophy," he said; "it is nothing new. I am perfectly familiar with it."

Yet this man was continually allowing himself to grow angry over the least trifle; he was quick to see and speak of the faults in others; he was demanding more of those he associated with in the way of consideration and justice than he was willing to give, and he was untidy in his person and improvident in his use of money.

Now it is the merest waste of time for this man to read "New Thought" literature or practice "deep breathing", since he will not put into daily and hourly practice what is taught by the New Religion.

He is like the orthodox Christian who mumbles through the Lord's Prayer and then goes forth to do exactly as he would not be done by in business, social and domestic life.

Man is what he thinks. Not what he says, reads or hears. By persistent thinking you can undo any condition which exists. You can free yourself from any chains, whether of poverty, sin, ill health or unhappiness. If you have been thinking these thoughts half a lifetime you must not expect to batter down the walls you have built, in a week, or a month, or a year. You must work and wait, and grow discouraged and stumble and pick yourself up and go on again.

You cannot in an hour gain control over a temper which you have let fly loose for twenty years. But you can control it eventually, and learn to think of a burst of anger as a vulgarity like drunkenness or profanity, something you could not descend to.

If you have allowed yourself to think despondent thoughts and believe that poverty and sickness were your portion for years, it will take time to train your mind to more cheerful and hopeful ideas; but you can do it by repeated assertions and by reading and thinking and living the beautiful New Thought Philosophy.

Optimism

Not long ago I read the following gloomy bit of pessimism from the pen of a man bright enough to know better than to add to the mental malaria of the world. He said:

Life is a hopeless battle in which we are foredoomed to defeat. And the prize for which we strive "to have and to hold", what is it? A thing that is neither enjoyed while had, nor missed when lost. So worthless it is, so unsatisfying, so inadequate to purpose, so false to hope and at its best so brief, that for consolation and compensation we set up fantastic faiths of an aftertime in a better world from which no confirming whisper has ever reached us out of the void. Heaven is a prophecy uttered by the lips of despair, but Hell is an inference from history.

This is morbid and unwholesome talk which can do no human being any good to utter, or listen to.

But it can depress and discourage the weak and struggling souls, who are striving to make the best of circumstances, and it can nerve to suicide the hand of some half-crazed being, who needed only a word of encouragement and cheer to brace up and win the race.

This is the unpardonable sin, to talk discouragingly to human souls, hungering for hope.

When the man without brains does it, he can be pardoned for knowing no better.

When the man with brains does it, he should be ashamed to look his fellow mortals in the eyes.

It is a sin ten times deeper dyed than giving a stone to those who ask for bread.

It is giving poison to those who plead for a cup of cold water.

Fortunately the remarks above quoted contain not one atom of truth!

The writer may speak for himself, but he has no right to speak for others.

It is all very well for a man who is marked with smallpox to say his face has not one unscarred inch on the surface of it. But he has no premises to stand upon when he says there is not a face in the world which is free from smallpox scars.

Life is not "a hopeless battle in which we are doomed to defeat."

Life is a glorious privilege, and we can make anything we choose of it, if we begin early and are in deep earnest, and realize our own divine powers.

Nothing can hinder us or stay us. We can do and be whatsoever we will.

The prize of life is not "a thing which is neither enjoyed while had nor missed when lost."

It is enjoyed by millions of souls to-day, this great prize of life. I for one declare that for every day of misery in my existence I have had a week of joy and happiness. For every hour of pain, I have had a day of pleasure. For every moment of worry, an hour of content.

I cannot be the only soul so endowed with the appreciation of life! I know scores of happy people who enjoy the many delights of earth, and there are thousands whom I do not know.

Of course "life is not missed when lost", because it is never lost. It is indestructible.

Life ever was, and ever will be. It is a continuous performance.

It is not "worthless" to the wholesome, normal mind. It is full of interest, and rich with opportunities for usefulness.

When any man says his life is worthless, it is because he has eyes and sees not, and ears and hears not.

It is his own fault, not the fault of God, fate or accident.

If every life seems at times "unsatisfactory" and "inadequate" it is only due to the cry of the immortal soul longing for larger opportunities and fewer limitations.

Neither is life "false to hope." He who trusts the divine Source of Life, shall find his hopes more than realized here upon earth. I but voice the knowledge of thousands of souls, when I make this assertion. I know whereof I speak.

All that our dearest hopes desire will come to us, if we believe in ourselves as rightful heirs to Divine Opulence, and work and think always on those lines.

If "no whisper has ever reached us out of the void" confirming our faith in immortality, then one-third of the seemingly intelligent and sane beings of our acquaintance must be fools or liars. For we have the assertion of fully this number that such whispers have come, besides the Biblical statistics of numerous messages from the other realm. "As it was in the beginning, is now and shall be ever more, world without end, Amen."

Preparation

Every day I hear middle-aged people bemoaning the fact that they were not given advantages or did not seize the opportunities for an education in early youth.

They believe that their lives would be happier, better and more useful had an education been obtained.

Scarcely one of these people realizes that middle life is the schooltime for old age, and that just as important an opportunity is being missed or ignored day by day for the storing up of valuable knowledge which will be of great importance in rendering old age endurable.

Youth is the season to acquire knowledge, middle life is the time to acquire wisdom.

Old age is the season to enjoy both, but wisdom is far the more important of the two.

By wisdom I mean the philosophy which enables us to control our tempers, curb our tendency to severe criticism, and cultivate our sympathies.

The majority of people after thirty-five consider themselves privileged to be cross, irritable, critical and severe, because they have lived longer than the young, because they have had more trials and disappointments, and because they believe they understand the world better.

Those are excellent reasons why they should be patient, kind, broad and sympathetic.

The longer we live the more we should realize the folly and vulgarity of ill temper, the cruelty of severe criticism and the necessity for a broad-minded view of life, manners, morals and customs.

Unless we adapt ourselves to the changing habits of the world, unless we adopt some of the new ideas that are constantly coming to the front, we will find ourselves carping, disagreeable and lonely old people as the years go by.

The world will not stand still for us. Society will not wear the same clothes or follow the same pleasures, or think the same thoughts when we are eighty that were prevalent when we were thirty. We must keep moving with the world or stand still and solitary.

After thirty we must seize every hour and educate ourselves to grow into agreeable old age.

It requires at least twenty years to become well educated in book and college lore. If we begin to study at seven we are rarely through with all our common schools, seminaries, high schools and colleges have to offer under a score of years.

The education for old age needs fully as many years. We need to begin at thirty to be tolerant, patient, serene, trustful, sympathetic and liberal. Then, at fifty, we may hope to have "graduated with honors" from life's school of wisdom, and to be prepared for another score or two of years of usefulness and enjoyment in the practice of these qualities.

Instead of wasting our time in bemoaning the loss of early opportunities for obtaining an education, let us devote ourselves to the cultivation of wisdom, since that is free to all who possess self-control, will power, faith and perseverance.

Begin to-day, at home. Be more tolerant of the faults of the other members of your household. Restrain your criticisms on the conduct of your neighbors.

Try and realize the causes which led some people who have gone wrong to err. Look for the admirable qualities in every one you meet. Sympathize with the world. Be interested in progress, be interested in the young. Keep in touch with each new generation, and do not allow yourself to grow old in thought or feeling.

Educate yourself for a charming old age. There is no time to lose.

Dividends

Our thoughts are shaping unmade spheres,
And, like a blessing or a curse,
They thunder down the formless years
And ring throughout the universe.

The more we realize the tremendous responsibility of our mental emanations the better for the world and ourselves. The sooner we teach little children what a mighty truth lies in the Bible phrase "As a man thinketh, so is he," the better for future generations.

If a man thinks sickness, poverty and misfortune, he will meet them and claim them all eventually as his own. But he will not acknowledge the close relationship, he will deny his own children and declare they were sent to him by an evil fate.

Walter Atkinson tells us that "he who hates is an assassin."

Every kindergarten and public school teacher ought to embody this idea in the daily lessons for children.

It may not be possible to teach a child to "love every neighbor as himself," for that is the most difficult of Commandments to follow to the letter; but it is possible to eliminate hatred from a nature if we awaken sympathy for the object of dislike.

That which we pity we cannot hate. The wonderful Intelligence which set this superb system of worlds in action must have been inspired by love for all it created.

So much grandeur and magnificence, so much perfection of detail, could only spring from Love.

Whatever is out of harmony in our little world has been caused by man's substituting hate and fear for love and faith.

Every time we allow either hate or fear to dominate our minds we disarrange the order of the universe and make trouble for humanity, and ourselves.

It may be a little late in reaching us, but it is sure to come back to the Mind which sent forth the cause.

Every time we entertain thoughts of love, sympathy, forgiveness and faith we add to the well-being of the world, and create fortunate and successful conditions for ourselves.

Those, too, may be late in coming to us BUT THEY WILL COME.

Right thinking is not attained in a day or a week.

We must train the mind to reject the brood of despondent, resentful, fearful and prejudiced thoughts which approach it, and to invite and entertain cheerful, broad and wholesome thoughts instead, just as we overcome false tones and cultivate musical ones in educating the voice for singing.

When we once realize that by driving away pessimistic, angry and bitter thoughts we drive away sickness and misfortune to a great extent, and that by seeking the kinder and happier frame of mind we seek at the same time success and health and good luck, we will find a new impetus in the control of our mental forces.

For we all love to be paid for our worthy deeds, even while we believe in being good for good's sake only. And nothing in life is surer than this:

RIGHT THINKING PAYS LARGE DIVIDENDS.

Think success, prosperity, usefulness. It is much more profitable than thinking self-destruction or the effort at self-destruction for that is an act which aims at an impossibility. You can destroy the body, but the you who suffers in mind and spirit will suffer still, and live still. You will only change your location from one state to another. You did not make yourself, you cannot unmake yourself. You can merely put yourself among the spiritual tramps who hang about the earth's borders, because they have not prepared a better place for themselves.

Suicide is cheap, vulgar and cowardly. Because you have made a wreck of a portion of this life, do not make a wreck of the next.

Mend up your broken life here, go along bravely and with sympathy and love in your heart, determined to help everybody you can, and to better your condition as soon as possible. Men have done this after fifty, and lived thirty good years to enjoy the results.

Do not feel hurt by the people who slight you, or who refer to your erring past. Be sorry for them. I would rather be a tender-hearted reformed sinner than a hard-hearted model of good behavior.

I would rather learn sympathy through sin than never learn it at all.

There is nothing we cannot live down, and rise above, and overcome. There is nothing we cannot be in the way of nobility and worth.

Royalty

We get what we give. I have never known this rule to fail in the long run. If we give sympathy, appreciation, goodwill, charitable thoughts, admiration and love, we receive all these back from humanity in time.

We may bestow them unworthily, as the sower of good seed may cast it on a rocky surface, but the winds of heaven will scatter it broadcast, and, while the rock remains barren, the fields shall yield a golden harvest.

The seed must be good, however.

If I say to myself without any real regard for another in my heart, "I want that person to like me, I will do all in my power to please him," I need not be surprised if my efforts fail or prove of only temporary efficacy.

Neither need I feel surprised or pained if I find by-and-by that other people are bestowing policy friendship upon me, actions with no feeling for a foundation.

No matter how kind and useful I make my conduct toward an individual, if in my secret heart I am criticising him severely and condemning him, I must expect criticism and condemnation from others as my portion.

We reap what we sow. Some harvests are longer in growing than others, but they all grow in time.

Servility in love, or friendship, or duty, is never commendable. I do not believe God Himself feels complimented when the beings He created as the highest type of His workmanship declare themselves worthless worms, unworthy of His regard!

We are heirs of God's kingdom, and rightful inheritors of happiness, and health, and success. What monarch would feel pleasure in having his children crawl in the dust, saying, "We are less than nothing, miserable, unworthy creatures?"

Would he not prefer to hear them say, proudly: "We are of royal blood"?

We ought always to believe in our best selves, in our right to love and be loved, to give and receive happiness, and to toil and be rewarded. And then we should bestow our love, our gifts and our toil with no anxious thought about the returns. If we chance to love a loveless individual, to give to one bankrupt in gratitude, to toil for the unappreciative, it is but a temporary deprivation for us. The love, the gratitude and the recompense will all come to us in time from some source, or many sources. It cannot fail.

Heredity

American parents, as a rule, can be put in two extreme classes, those who render the children insufferably conceited and unbearable by overestimating their abilities and overpraising their achievements, and those who render them morbid and self-depreciating by a lack of wholesome praise.

It is rare indeed, when we find parents wise and sensible enough to strengthen the best that is in their children by discreet praise, and at the same time to control the undesirable qualities by judicious and kind criticism.

I heard a grandmother not long ago telling callers in the presence of a small boy what a naughty, bad child he was, and how impossible it seemed to make him mind. Wretched seed to sow in the little mind, and the harvest is sure to be sorrow.

I have heard parents and older children, expatiate on the one stupid trait and the one plain feature of a bright and handsome child, intending to keep it from forming too good an opinion of itself.

To all young people I would say, cultivate a belief in yourself. Base it on self-respect and confidence in God's love for his own handiwork. Say to yourself, "I will be what I will to be." Not because your human will is all-powerful, but because the Divine will is back of you. Analyze your own abilities and find what you are best fitted to do.

Then get about the task of doing your chosen work to the very best of your ability, and do not for an instant doubt your own capabilities. Perhaps they may be dwarfed and enfeebled by years of morbid thought; but if you persist in a self-respecting and self-reliant and God-trusting course of thinking your powers will increase and your capabilities strengthen.

It is no easy matter to overcome a habit of self-depreciation.

It is like straightening out a limb which has been twisted by a false attitude or correcting a habit of sitting round-shouldered.

It requires a steady and persistent effort. When the depressing and doubtful thoughts come drive them away like malaria-breeding insects. Say, "This is not complimentary to my Maker. I am His work. I must be worthy of my own respect and of that of others. I must and will succeed."

Invincibility

If we persistently desire good things to come to us for unselfish purposes, and at the same time faithfully perform the duties which lie nearest, we will eventually find our desires being realized in the most unexpected manner.

Our thought force has proved to be a wedge, opening the seemingly inaccessible Wall of Circumstance.

To read good books, to think and ponder on what you read, to cultivate every agreeable quality you observe in others, and to weed from your nature every unworthy and disagreeable trait, to study humanity with an idea of being helpful and sympathetic, all these efforts will help you to the ultimate attainment of your wishes.

It is a proven fact that if we devote a few moments each day to reaching exercises, standing with loose garments and stretching the body muscles to reach some point above us, we increase our stature.

Just so if we mentally and spiritually are continually reaching to a higher plane we are growing.

Every least thought of the brain is a chisel, chipping away at our characters, and our characters are building our destinies.

The incessant and persistent demand of our hearts and minds MUST be granted.

That Mental Chisel

During a trolley ride through a thrifty New England locality, where church spires were almost as plentiful as trees, I studied the faces of the people who came into the car during my two hours' journey.

The day was beautiful, and all along the route our numbers were recruited by bevies of women, young, middle aged and old, who were bent on shopping expeditions or setting forth to make social calls.

They went and came at each village through which our coach of democracy passed, and they represented all classes.

The young girls were lovely, as young girls are the world over: their complexion possessed that soft tender luster, peculiar to seashore localities, for the salty breath of Father Neptune is the greatest of cosmetics. Many of the young faces were formed in classic mould, their features clearly cut and refined, and severe, like the thoughts and principles of their ancestors.

Often I observed a mother and some female relative, presumably an aunt, in company with a young relative; and always the sharpening and withering process of the years of set and unelastic thought was discernible upon their faces, which had once been young, and classic and attractive.

In the entire two hours I saw but three lovely faces which were matured by time.

I saw scores of well-dressed and evidently well-cared-for women of middle age, whose countenances were furrowed, drawn, pinched, sallow, and worn, beyond excuse; for time, sorrow, and sickness are not plausible excuses for such ravages upon a face God drew in lines of beauty.

Time should mature a woman's beauty as it does that of a tree. Sorrow should glorify it as does the frost the tree, and sickness should not be allowed to lay a lingering touch upon it, until death calls the spirit away.

Without question the great majority of the women I saw were earnest orthodox Christians.

I heard snatches of conversation regarding Church and Charities and I have no doubt that each woman among them believed herself to be a disciple of Christ.

Yet where was the result of the loving, tender, sweet spirit of Christ's teaching?

It surely was not visible upon those pinched and worried faces? And those faces were certain and truthful chronicles of the work done by the minds within.

One face said to me in every line, "I talk about God's goodness and loving-kindness, but I worry over the dust in the spare room, I fret about our expenses, I am troubled about my lungs, and I fear my husband has an unregenerate heart. I never know an hour's peace, for even in my sleep, I worry, worry, worry, but of course I know I will be saved by the blood of Christ!"

Another said, "I am in God's fold, well and safe, but I hate and despise my nearest neighbor, for she wears clothes that I am sure she cannot pay for, and her children are always dressed better than mine. I quarrel with my domestics, and am always in trouble of some kind, just because human beings are so full of sin and no one but myself is ever right. I shall be so glad to leave this world of woe and go to heaven, but I hope I will not meet many of my present acquaintances there!"

Another said, "If I only had good health but I was born to sickness and suffering, and it is God's will that I should suffer!"

Oh the pity of it, and to imagine this is religion!

Thank God the wave of "New Thought" is sweeping over the land, and washing away those old blasphemous errors of mistaken creeds.

The "New Thought" is to give us a new race of beautiful middle-aged and old people.

To-day in any part of the land among rich, poor, ignorant or intellectual, orthodox or materialists the beautiful mature face is rarer than a white blackbird in the woods.

It is impossible to be plain, ugly, or uninteresting in late life, if the mind keeps itself occupied with right thinking.

The withered and drawn face of fifty indicates withered emotions and drawn and perverted ambitions.

The dried and sallow face tells its story of dried up sympathies and hopes.

The furrowed face tells of acid cares eating into the heart.

All this is irreligious! yet all this prevails extensively in our most conservative and churchy communities.

He who in truth trusts God cannot worry.

He who loves God and mankind, cannot become dried and withered at fifty, for love will re-create his blood, and renew the fires of his eye.

He who understands his own divine nature will grow more beautiful with the passing of time, for the God within will become each year more visible.

The really reverent soul accepts its sorrows as blessings in disguise, and he who so accepts them is beautified and glorified by them, within and without.

Are you growing more attractive as you advance in life? Is your eye softer and deeper, is your mouth kinder, your expression more sympathetic, or are you screwing up your face in tense knots of worry? Are your eyes growing hopeless and dull, is your mouth drooping at the corners, and becoming a set thin line in the centre, and is your skin dry, and sallow, and parched?

Study yourself and answer these questions to your own soul, for in the answer depends the decision whether you really love and trust God, and believe in your own immortal spirit, or whether you are a mere impostor in the court of faith.

The Object of Life

What do you believe to be the object of your life?

To be happy and successful, perhaps you are thinking, even if you do not answer in those words.

That is the idea of the many. Meanwhile others, who have been educated in the melancholy faith of their ancestors, believe the object of this life is to be miserable, poor, and full of sorrow, that they may wear a crown of glory hereafter.

But the clear thinker and careful observer must realize that there is one and only one main object in life; the building of character.

He who sets out in early youth with that ambition and purpose, and keeps to it, will not only attain his object, but he will, too, attain happiness and true success, for there is no such thing as failure for the man or woman of character.

We often apply the two words character and success, unworthily.

We speak of a man of "much character" when he is merely self-assertive and stubborn, and we call a man successful, who has accumulated a fortune, or achieved fame and a position, by doubtful methods.

Then what is character, and what is success?

Character is the result of the cultivation of the highest and noblest qualities in human nature, and putting those qualities to practical use.

Success is the conquest of the lower and baser self, and the ability to be useful to one's fellow men.

There are men of brain, wealth and position who are failures, and there are men of limited abilities and in humble places who are yet successful, inasmuch as they make the utmost of themselves, and their opportunities.

It makes no difference how lowly your sphere in life may be, and no matter how limited your environment, you can build your character if you will. You need no outlay of money, no assistance from those in power, no influence.

Character Building must be done alone, and by yourself. The ground must be cleansed of debris, and the structure must be erected stone by stone.

It is dull, slow, hard work, especially the preparation.

All preparation is drudgery.

When this little whirling globe of ours began to cool in space think what a task lay before it! Think of the mass of chaos, which had to slowly shape itself into mighty, green, glad and snow-capped mountains, fertile vales, and noble forests.

Each one of us is a little world, whirling alone on an individual orbit, but the divine power is within us, to grow into symmetry, beauty, and perfection if we only realize it.

And the happiness of the work, once we begin it, is beyond the power of description.

There is no other satisfaction can compare with that of looking back across the years and finding that you have grown in self-control, in charity of judgment, in a sense of justice, in generosity, and in unselfishness.

If you are conscious of this growth, let no lack of material success for one moment disturb you. That will come, enough for your need, in time.

The man of symmetrically developed character is never a pauper.

He is never dependent for more than a temporary period.

To possess character is to be useful, and to be useful is to be independent, and to be useful and independent, is to be happy, even in the midst of sorrow; for sorrow is not necessarily unhappiness.

The man who has made the development of a noble and harmonious character the business of his life, accepts his sorrows as means of greater growth, and finds in them an exaltation of spirit which is closely allied to happiness.

To such a nature, absolute wretchedness would only be possible through the loss of self-respect; the lowering of an ideal or the failure of a principle.

Would you be happy and successful? Then set yourself to build character.

Seek to be worthy of your own highest commendation.

Wisdom

A great many people are attracted to the New Thought of the day, by its declaration of our right to material wealth, and by its claim that the mind of man can create, command, and control conditions which produce wealth.

There is no question concerning the truth of this claim.

But woe unto him who cultivates his mental and spiritual powers only for this purpose.

His gold shall turn to dross, his pleasure to Dead Sea fruit.

He shall be as one who drags a beautiful garment through the mud of the streets, and while clothed in purple and fine linen is yet a repulsive object.

Into the Great Scheme of Existence, as first conceived by the Creator, money did not enter.

He made this beautiful Universe, and all that it contains was meant for the enjoyment of His creatures.

There was no millionaire and no pauper soul created by God.

Each soul contains the spark of the divine spirit, and by the realization of that spark, and all it means, whatever is desired by mortal man may come to him.

But wise is he who remembers the injunction, "Seek first the kingdom of heaven and all other things shall be added unto you."

Wise is he who understands the meaning of the words, "Unto him that hath, more shall be given."

Not until you obtain the faculty of being happy through your spiritual and mental faculties, independent of material conditions, not until you learn to value wealth only as a means of helpfulness, can you safely turn your powers of concentration upon the idea of opulence.

To demand, assert, and command wealth for its mere sensual benefits, to focus your mind upon it because you desire to shine, lead, and triumph, is to play spiritual football with spiritual dynamite.

You may obtain what you seek, you may accumulate riches, but at the cost of all that is worth living for.

The merely ignorant, or stupid, or wholly material man who stumbles into a fortune, through inheritance, dogged persistent industry, or chance, may enjoy it in his own fashion, and do no harm in the world.

But the man who knows and who has developed his spiritual powers only for the purpose of commanding material gain, might better have a millstone tied about his neck. For he makes himself a spiritual outcast, and his money shall never bring him happiness.

Make, therefore, your assertion of opulence the last in your list, as you make Love first.

Call unto yourself spiritual insight, absolute unselfishness, desire for universal good, wisdom, justice, and usefulness, and last of all opulence.

Think of yourself as possessed of all these qualities before you picture financial independence.

For without love for your kind, without the desire for usefulness and the spiritual insight and the wisdom to be just before being generous, your money would bring you only temporary pleasure, and would do the world no good.

Neither should you labor under the impression that God's work is lying undone because you have no fortune to command and wisely distribute where most needed. Rest assured if you do the work which lies nearest to you, relieve such distress as is possible to you, and keep your faith in the ultimate justice of God's ways, that the world will move on, and humanity will slowly attain its destined goal, even if you never become a millionaire.

Self Conquest

Every New Idea, or supposed New Idea, is a light which attracts the moths.

The "New Thought" is no exception.

About it flutter hysterical women, unbalanced men: the erratic and the irresponsible.

The possibilities of performing miracles, of healing the sick, hypnotizing the well, transforming poverty into wealth, and changing age to youth, are the rays of light which flicker through the darkness and draw them into the circle of radiance.

The self-indulgent fat woman subscribes to New Thought literature, pays for a course of lectures, and goes forth into the ranks of the unbelievers, proclaiming her power to become a sylph, and to cause others to become sylphs.

The extravagant and inconsiderate rush forth after having heard a discourse upon the power of mind over matter, and declare that they possess the secret of accumulating a fortune by occult means.

The lovers of the marvelous believe that they will become great healers in a brief space of time.

Not one of these moth converts realizes that the very first step to take in the direction of "New Thought" is self-conquest.

The gourmand does not know that self-indulgence and a gross appetite are incompatible with mental or spiritual growth, and will be insurmountable obstacles in her path toward symmetry.

The spendthrift does not take into consideration the fact that good sense, thrift and industry, must aid his mental assertion of wealth, and the miracle lover does not understand that something greater and more difficult is required than a mere wish to heal before healing powers can be obtained.

That the physical body and material conditions can be dominated by the divine spirit in man, is an incontrovertible fact.

But first, last and always, the lesser self must be subjugated, and the weak and unworthy qualities overcome.

The woman who desires to reduce her flesh cannot do so by reading occult literature, or joining mystic circles, or attending lectures, unless she permeates herself so thoroughly with spiritual truths that she no longer craves six courses at dinner, and three meals a day, and unless she overcomes her dislike for exercise.

The man who wishes to control circumstances must love better things than money before he can succeed. He must love, and respect, and believe in his Creator, and trust the Divine Man within himself, and he must illustrate this love and trust by his daily conduct, and in his home circle, and in his business relations.

Once in a century, perhaps, is a man born with great powers already developed to heal the sick, or to do other seeming miracles. Such beings are old souls, who have obtained diplomas in former lives; but the majority of us are still in school, and we cannot become "seniors" until we pass through the lower grades.

We must change ourselves before we can change material conditions: we must heal our own thoughts and make them sane and normal, before we can heal bodily disease in others.

It is not an immediate process. I have heard an old lady declare that she "got religion" in the twinkling of an eye, and she believed all people would be damned and burn in hell fire, who did not pass through this sudden illumination.

It is possible that the religion which can worship a God cruel enough to burn his children in fire, can only be obtained in the twinkling of an eye; but the reverent, wholesome, and beautiful religion of "New Thought" must be grown into little by little, through patience, faith, and practice.

All that it claims to do it can do, but not instantaneously, not rapidly. We must first make ourselves over; after absolute control of our minds has been obtained, then, and only then, may we hope to influence circumstances and health.

The Important Trifles

You will find, in the effort to reach a higher spirituality in your daily life, that the small things try your patience and your strength more than the greater ones.

Home life, like business life, is composed of an accumulation of trifles.

There are people who bear great sorrows with resignation, and seem to gain a certain dignity and force of character through trouble, but who are utterly vanquished by trivial annoyances.

The old-fashioned orthodox "Christian" was frequently of this order.

Death, poverty, and misfortune he bore without complaining, and became ofttimes a more agreeable companion in times of deepest sorrow.

He regarded all such experiences as the will of God, and bowed to them.

Yet, if his dinner was late, his coffee below the standard, if his eyeglasses were misplaced, or his toe trodden upon, he become a raging lion, and his roar drove his affrighted household into dark corners.

There have been neighborhood Angels, who watched beside the dying sinner, sustained orphans and widows, and endured great troubles sublimely like martyrs. But if a dusty shoe trod upon a freshly washed floor, or husband or child came tardily to the breakfast-table, or lingered outside the door after regulation hour for retiring, lo, the Angel became a virago, or a droning mosquito with persistent sting.

The New Philosophy demands serenity and patience through small trials, as well as fortitude in meeting life's larger ills.

It demands, too, that we seek to avoid giving others unnecessary irritation by a thoughtless disregard of the importance of trifles.

A man is more likely to keep calm if he wakes in the night and discovers that the house is on fire, than he is if, on being fully prepared to retire, he finds the only mug on the third story is missing from his wash-stand, or the cake of toilet-soap he asked for the day before has been forgotten.

A mother bears the affliction of a crippled child with more equanimity than she is able to bring to bear upon the continual thoughtlessness of a strong one.

To be kind, means to be thoughtful.

The kindest and most loving heart will sometimes forget and be careless; but it cannot be perpetually forgetful and careless of another's wishes and needs, even in the merest trifles.

Concentration

The New Thought includes concentration of thought, in its teaching; and he who learns that important art is not liable to frequently forget small or large duties.

It is he who scatters, instead of concentrates his mind powers, who keeps himself and others in a state of continual irritation by forgetting, mislaying, and losing, three petty vices which do much to mar domestic or business life.

Concentration is a most difficult acquirement for the mature mind which has been allowed to grow in the habit of thought scattering.

Wise is the mother, and as sure as wise, who teaches her child to finish each task begun before attempting another, for that is the first step in concentration.

Prentice Mulford, that great and good pioneer in the field of practical New Thought, tells us to apply our whole mental powers to whatever we do, even if it is merely the tying of a shoe, and to think of nothing else until that shoe is tied, then to utterly forget the shoe string, when we turn to another duty or employment. The next lesson in concentration he gives us, is to repeat the word often, to impress it upon the mind.

And then to declare each day that "Concentration is mine" will aid still farther in the acquisition of this great and important quality.

Meanwhile, since we can be so fortunate as to always surround ourselves with others who have acquired it, the student of the Higher Philosophy must learn to be serene and self-poised when he encounters life's pigmy worries.

He must carry his religion into his bedroom and his office, and not forget it utterly when he loses his collar-button, or misses his car, or finds his office boy has taken a parcel to the wrong address.

To build character necessitates a constant watch upon ourselves. The New Thought is not a religion of Sundays, but of every day.

Destiny

Never say that you wish your situation were different! Never wish you had some other person's life or troubles or worries.

Accept your own as a working basis, the best for you.

Then go ahead and change whatever displeases you.

Remember you are the maker and moulder of your own destiny. You do not recall the fact, but you brought about the present conditions of your destiny in former incarnations.

Even if you do not believe this, you must acknowledge that you are here, and that the situation in which you find yourself seems to be inevitable for the present.

But it is not inevitable for the future, unless you lie down in the furrow and whine, and wish you were a millionaire, or a genius, and rail at the partiality of Providence.

There is no partiality in the Universe.

The whole scheme is well balanced. If you were allowed to change lots with anyone on the face of the earth, you would complain and find fault in a short time.

One of our best known millionaires, born to opulence, complains that he has been robbed of the privilege of making his own fortune.

He is no happier than you. His confession betrays his weakness of character just as your repining and fault-finding betrays yours.

The real worth-while character thanks God for its destiny and says, "I will show the world what I can do with my life."

Not long ago there was a great trotting-race at Brighton Beach. The blind conqueror "Rythmic" won five consecutive races.

Think of it! He did not, like a mortal man, shrink back and say "I am blind, that is a terrible destiny, I am cursed of God, I will not try to win the race." He just trusted the hand of the Master at the reins, did his best, and won the honors of the season.

We are all blind racers on the track of earth. The king, the millionaire, the statesman, the lawmaker, the beggar, the laborer, the cripple, we are all in the dark. The only thing is to trust the hand of the Master, and do our best.

Believe your position is the right starting point for you, merely the starting point.

It is the shapeless block of stone from which you are to fashion the perfect statue.

Or it is the mere mud from which you are to mould the clay image, and later that is to be put into enduring marble.

What is uglier or more unattractive than mud?

Yet think of the glorious conceptions which it imprisons.

Take the mud of your present environment and thank God for it, and make the image of the future you desire.

You can do it, you must do it, you will do it.

Sympathy

Are you of a sympathetic nature?

If so, do not let your sympathies help to add to the world's miseries.

That may seem a strange expression, but it can be explained if you will listen.

Much of the misery in the world is the result of imagination.

All of it is the result of selfishness and ignorance.

But hundreds and thousands of people believe themselves sick, sorrowful and poverty stricken, who would be well, glad and prosperous, if they only thought themselves so.

Every time you pour out your sympathy upon these self-made sufferers, you add to their burden of wrong thought, and make it just so much more difficult for them to rise out of their troubles.

I do not believe all the misfortune in the world is caused by wrong thinking in this life, or can be done away with by right thinking. The three-year-old child who toddles in front of a trolley car and loses a leg, while the tired mother is bending over the washtub to keep the wolf of hunger at bay, cannot be blamed for wrong thinking as the cause of its trouble. Neither can the deaf mute or the child born blind or deformed. We must go farther back, to former lives, to find the first cause of such misfortunes.

No "New Thought," no amount of optimistic theology or philosophy can restore the child's leg, or ears, or eyes. It is utter nonsense to say that miracles like these can be performed.

There are scores of individuals whom we meet handicapped in life's race by such dire calamities that we spontaneously pour forth our sympathy.

But, even to these, it were kinder and wiser to give diverting thoughts, and a new outlook, and to open up avenues for pleasure, and entertainment, and profit, in place of tears and condolence.

Sympathy, without alleviating actions to a sufferer, is like a cloud without rain to the parched earth.

But the great majority of people whom we encounter are making their own crosses, and we who offer them sympathy, and condolence, are but adding to the burden's weight.

I do not recommend coldness, indifference, or ridicule as a substitute for sympathy. But instead of leading the sick man on to tell you the details of his illness, and to describe all his symptoms, while your own body responds with sympathetic aches and pains as you listen, it is kinder to divert his attention to some cheerful and merry topic, or to refer to some case like his own which resulted in perfect restoration to health. Instead of going down into his underground cave of depression, bring him out into the wholesome sunlight of your own healthful state, even if for a moment only, and impress upon his mind that health belongs to him, and must return to him.

To the man in business trouble the same advice applies.

Tell him you are sorry for him, but do not take on his despondency to prove it.

Talk of the future and all the possibilities it holds for a determined man or woman.

Make him laugh. Speak of trouble as the gymnasium where our moral muscles are developed. Answer him that everything he desires is his if he will be persistent and determined in demanding his own. If you put force in your words you will leave an impression.

Do not go away from the house of trouble in tears, but leave the troubled ones you called upon smiling as you depart.

That is true sympathy.

The Breath

A man reproved me for my interest in New Thought creeds.

"The old religion I learned at my mother's knee is good enough for me!" he said. "It is good enough for anybody!"

Yet this man's mother had always "enjoyed poor health," as the old lady expressed it, and the man himself was forever talking of his diseases, his ill luck, his poverty, which he said he had been enabled to endure only through the sustaining power of the religion "learned at his mother's knee."

It would be difficult to convince the man that had his mother taught him the creed of the "New Religion" he could have changed all these unfortunate conditions.

Life-long ill health would have been impossible for his mother, or for him.

The old fashioned religion allowed and still allows a human being to breathe like a canary bird.

Little children go to Sunday-School all their young lives, and grow up to be devout church members, and never hear one word about the importance of deep breathing.

Possibly you may think breathing lessons belong to physical culture, and have no place in religious teachings.

There is where you err.

In order to develop your whole being, you must learn how to control body and mind through the spirit.

Thousands of years ago, men who gave their entire lives to the study of these things learned the great importance of deep breathing as an aid to religious meditation.

By this practice, systematically observed, the body is calmed, the mind is brought into subjection, and the spirit rises into control.

And in addition, absolute health is achieved.

A large portion of our physical ailments result from unused lung cells, and consequent imperfect circulation of the blood.

Fill the lungs full, every cell, with fresh air, two or three times daily, and do not overload the digestive organs, and sickness will fly away to the dark regions where it belongs.

At least ten minutes morning and night should be given to the breathing exercises.

Sit upright in a comfortable chair, alone, facing the east in the morning and the west at night, because great magnetic force comes from the direction of the sun.

Have a window or a door opening to the outer air.

Place your hands lightly on your knees, and close your eyes and mouth. Leave your spine free, not touching the chair. Wear no compressing garments or bands.

Inflate the chest and abdominal regions as you inhale deep breaths through the nostrils, while counting seven slowly.

Exhale while you count seven. Repeat this exercise seven times.

Think as you inhale of whatever qualities you would like to possess, and believe that you are inhaling them. Select seven qualities; Love, Health, Wisdom, Usefulness, Power to Do Good, Success, Opulence, will cover the average human desires. The very unworldly will substitute spiritual knowledge for opulence. Fill your mind with the idea that you are drawing in these qualities with your breaths, and exhaling all that is weak or unworthy. After a few moments you will be conscious of a security and peace new and uplifting.

And after a few weeks of steady, persistent practice of these exercises, you will find life growing more beautiful to you, and your strength will be increased tenfold, both physically and spiritually.

Generosity

Have you ever observed how invariably your "last dollar" is restored to you, with additions, when you have given it for some worthy purpose?

Even if the purpose did not prove to be a worthy one, yet if you thought it so, and gave your last dollar with spontaneous sympathy and good will, you were not long left penniless.

Money is much like a man. If you do not hold it too jealously it returns to you the more readily.

Never hesitate to give aid where you feel there is sore and pressing need, for fear you will be left in want yourself. You will not be.

This does not mean that indiscriminate charity is commendable. It does not mean that you should lend money to everyone who asks, or lift and carry the burdens of everyone who is ready to lean upon you.

It is as wrong to encourage the man addicted to the vice of borrowing, as the one with the vice of alcohol or drugs.

One depends upon his acquaintances to tide him over hard places, instead of upon his own strength of character, and the other depends upon stimulants for the same purpose. The too ready lender is almost as great an evil to humanity as rum or opium, since he too helps a man to kill his own better nature and destroy his self-respect.

If you were able and willing to pay rents of all the poor people you know, and clothe their children, you would soon produce a condition of settled pauperism among them. Large and frequent favors of a financial nature are an injury to anyone, even if it is your son or brother.

Let no man lean on anyone save God and his own divine self.

But little helps, when they are unexpected, arouse hope and awaken new faith and new ambition in a discouraged soul.

Look about you for such souls, the worn and weary father of a brood of hungry children, the widow struggling with adverse fate in an effort to clothe and educate a child, the tired shop girl who uses all her earnings to sustain her parents, the ambitious boy or girl eager for a chance in life, and the poor cripple or invalid seeking health. You will find them all about you. Do not be afraid to use a dollar here or there to give those worthy ones a happy surprise, no matter how poor you are.

It is an insult to the Opulent Creator to suppose you will suffer want and poverty if you help those who are in temporary misfortune.

You will not.

Ofttimes we read and hear of the open-handed generous man who helped everybody," and who "never refused to aid a needy brother," and who ended his life in penury because of his generosity.

Never believe these tales until you investigate them. Invariably you will find not generosity but extravagance and utter lack of forethought, caused the man's financial ruin.

I recall a gifted young woman who gave freely to all who asked her assistance and who died a lingering death as a charity patient in a hospital.

Yet this young woman had expended ten dollars on foolish and rapid living where she gave one in charity; it was her wasteful extravagance, not her open heart of sympathy, which made her a pauper.

It has been my observation that dollars planted in the soil of benevolence grow into harvests of prosperity. The man who is not afraid to use his small means to assist others need not fear poverty.

Woman's Opportunity

The greatest opportunity to better the world which can come to any woman is through the experience of maternity.

The power of prenatal influence which a mother possesses is awe-inspiring to realize.

It has been said upon excellent authority that Napoleon's mother read Roman history with absorbing interest during the months preceding his birth.

Think of the nations and the centuries influenced by that one woman's mental concentration! The geography of the world was changed by her power of focused thought.

In all probability Napoleon's mother did not know what she was doing; she was not conscious of the destiny her mind was shaping for her unborn child, nor of the law governing such conditions.

Women have been strangely ignorant of this vital truth; until recent years it has not been considered a "proper" theme for tongue or pen, and to-day the great majority of young women marry absolutely uninformed upon the subject of prenatal influence.

Men are equally oblivious of any knowledge regarding the matter, and consequently make no special effort to keep the expectant mother of their offspring happy, hopeful, or free of anxiety and worry during this period. Often they do not strive to aid them in their own attempts to bestow a desirable temperament upon the unborn child, but heedlessly and needlessly aggravate or grieve the mind which is stamping its impress upon an unborn soul.

It is just here that the "New Thought" can perform its greatest miracles of good.

Even the woman who has not been enlightened upon the law of ante-birth-influence will, if a true disciple of the Religion of Right-living, bring healthy and helpful children into the world, because her normal state of mind will be inclusive of those three qualities; and her continued and repeated assertions of her own divine nature will shape the brain of her child in optimistic and reverential mould.

There is the old law of the continual falling of the drop of water upon the stone to be verified in the spiritual plane. Continual assertions of a mother that her child will be all that she desires it to be, will wear away the stone of inherited tendencies, and bring into physical being a malleable nature wholly amenable to the after influences and efforts she may bring to bear upon it.

It is a tremendous responsibility which rests upon the woman who knows she is to be a mother of a human being.

A hundred ancestors may have contributed certain qualities to that invisible and formless atom which contains an immortal soul, yet the mother's mind has the power to remake and rebuild all those characteristics, and to place over them her own dominating impulse, whether for good or ill.

Surely, if success in the arts or the sciences is worthy of years of devoted attention and interested effort, the moulding of a noble human being is worth eight or nine months of concentrated thought and unflagging zeal of purpose.

Every expectant mother should set herself about the important business God has entrusted her with, unafraid, and confident of her divine mission. She should direct her mind into wholesome and optimistic channels; she should read inspiring books and think loving and large thoughts. She should pray and aspire! and always should she carry in her mind the ideal of the child she would mother, and command from the great Source of all Opulence the qualities she would desire to perpetuate.

And they will be given.

Balance

Avoid all strained and abstruse language, when conversing with people who may not have entered this realm of thought.

Do not allow anyone to think of you as a lunatic, or a crank, unnecessarily. Of course there are people in the world who consider everyone a lunatic who holds an opinion differing from their own.

But it can do you, or your philosophy, no good to thrust its most difficult phases before the minds of the unawakened, by vague and high flown expressions.

I once chanced to call upon a lady who had, quite unknown to me, entered upon the study of Christian Science.

She remarked to me, almost as soon as the greetings were exchanged, "I had a claim to meet for three days this week, but I have come through it and am victorious."

I supposed the lady referred to some business matter, perhaps a legal affair, and waited an explanation.

After considerable rambling conversation, I managed to grasp the fact that the woman had been sick in the house three days, but now was well. She considered her illness a mere "claim" her "mortal mind" had made which she had to meet and combat.

All this sort of talk is very ridiculous. We need not talk about every ailment which attacks us as we move along toward the condition of perfect health which belongs to us! But if we do speak of indisposition, let us use common sense language.

What we want to realize is, that we are in the body, but that the spirit can control bodily conditions, if we give it the ascendency, to the extent of keeping us well, moral, useful, and comfortable even in the midst of sickness, vice, indolence and poverty.

We can rise above these false elements, and subjugate them.

Meanwhile we cannot live without food, clothes and money.

Despise and ignore these vulgar things as we may assume to do, we yet must have them.

It brings only ridicule upon ourselves and our ideas to make this pretense of despising the necessities of life.

To make them secondary in our thoughts to spiritual knowledge is right and wise, but this is better illustrated by our lives and conduct than by our words.

Ella Wheeler Wilcox – A Short Biography

Ella Wheeler was born on 5th November, 1850, on a farm in the village of Johnstown, Rock County, Wisconsin. Her parents, Marcus H. Wheeler and Sarah Pratt Wheeler, already had three children. A year earlier the family had moved from Vermont after Marcus's attempts at show business failed and becoming a farmer was his response. With Ella's birth they moved again. This time further north to Madison.

Ella was a gifted child, writing poetry and novels from an early age. The family was poor but her parents believed in education, and whilst little could be afforded they helped as best they could most usefully with grammar, spelling and vocabulary. Her initial education was at the local district school in the village of Windsor, now re-named in her honour as Ella Wheeler Wilcox School.

During her thirteenth year subscriptions the family had been receiving from the New York Mercury, a popular periodical, ceased. This greatly upset her. Life on the farm was lonely and the magazine had been a source of comfort and information about the big world beyond the farm. The family could not afford its own subscription so Ella had to make other plans.

Her writing ambitions were central to this. She wrote two essays but now had to obtain stamps so she could get her submissions in front of editors. She was corresponding with a young girl, Jean, who was in the freshman class at Madison University. Assuring her friend of future payment she enclosed the letter and essays for the New York Mercury.

By 1866, Jean, at Ella's behest, sent a list of all the monthlies and weeklies on the newsstands and Ella was hard at work saving pennies for postage as she began to mail them en masse with her works. Quickly her family lent their support to help out with her endeavours. Ella's mother especially had always thought her daughter would be the one to find the fame, travel and recognition that she had wanted herself and seeing the efforts Ella was putting in she was only to glad to help.

Soon the house the house was filled with ALL the periodicals. Editors would send magazines, books, pictures, bric-a-brac and tableware in response to Ella's requests and works. Being able to earn these items brought her great satisfaction and honed her skills.

She remembers the period in her autobiography:

"The very first verses I sent for publication were unmercifully "guyed" by my beloved "Mercury." The editor urged me to keep to prose and to avoid any further attempts at rhyme. He said that, while this criticism would wound me temporarily, it would eventually confer a favour on me and the world at large.

"My first check came from Frank Leslie's publishing house. I wrote asking for one of his periodicals to be sent to me in return for three little poems I had composed in one day. In reply came a check for ten dollars, saying I must select which one of some thirteen publications they issued at that time.

This bit of crisp paper opened a perfect floodgate of aspiration, inspiration and ambition for me. I had not thought of earning money so soon. I had expected to obtain only books, magazines and articles of use and beauty from the editor's prize-lists; and I had not supposed verses to be saleable. I wrote them because they came to me, but I expected to be a novelist like Mrs. Southworth and May Agens Fleming in time - that was the goal of my dreams. The check from Leslie was a revelation. I walked, talked, thought and dreamed in verse after that. A day which passed without a poem from my pen I considered lost and misused. Two each day was my idea of industry, and I once achieved eight. They sold, the majority, for three dollars or five dollars each. Sometimes I got ten dollars for a poem, that was always an event. Short love-stories, over which I laboured painfully, as story writing was an acquired habit, also added to my income, bringing me ten or fifteen dollars, and once in a while larger sums, from "Peterson's," "Demorest's," "Harper's Bazaar" and the "Chimney Corner."

Ella was beginning to understand the route to success and had the work ethic and creativity to turn it to her advantage. Ella would write her daily quota of poems and other works and then send them out to editors in the hope of getting them published.

It was also about this time that she also left the Country school. Her record in grammar, spelling, reading had of course been excellent but she had a horror of mathematics preferring to spend as much time as possible in the world of her imagination. Ella's talent and determination was such that by now, after she graduated from High School she was already well known in her state as a young writer.

In this she was encouraged by her mother, who despised her own life and felt herself and her family superior to all her neighbours and was forever impressing on the young teenager that her life would blossom and she would achieve success as a writer.

In 1867 her parents sent her to Madison where she was a junior in the Female College, a part of the University of Wisconsin. Ella wanted to spend all of her time writing and begged to come home. She didn't feel the need for further education and was painfully aware of the difference between her homemade clothes and the dresses of city girl. These and other differences caused her to feel left out and not part of the group. After many requests her parents relented and she was allowed home to continue her writing.

In 1870 she was offered employment at $45 a month to edit the literary department of a publication by the magazine's Milwaukee Editor. She accepted, but the hours and work were not to her liking and after three months the magazine folded and her single experience of working in an office was over. Now she was to be a full time author.

In 1872 she published her first book. It was an unusual step as it was a book of poems entitled 'Drops Of Water: Poems' that were solely about abstinence. Published by the National Temperance society it reflected her views on the evils of alcohol and earned her a $50 fee.

She published further books over the next decade but it wasn't until 1883 and the rather racy, for those times, publication of Poems of Passion that her success moved suddenly forward. It was an immediate and large scale success selling over 60,000 in two years.

That same year was also noteworthy for she was engaged to be married. Robert Wilcox was one of many suitors to the young Ella. He was a silver salesman from Meriden, Connecticut. Although they only met three times before the wedding it was to be the relationship that defined her life and much of her work. They married the following year in 1884.

Her most famous poem, "Solitude", was first published on 25th February, 1883 in an issue of The New York Sun. The inspiration for the poem came as she was travelling to attend the State Governor's inaugural ball in Madison, Wisconsin. Whilst travelling to the celebration she was sitting next to a young woman, dressed in black, who was in obvious distress. Ella comforted her for the whole journey. Recalling the widow's emotional state Ella wrote:

Laugh, and the world laughs with you;
Weep, and you weep alone.
For the sad old earth must borrow its mirth
But has trouble enough of its own

She sent the poem to the Sun and received $5 for her effort. It was collected in the book Poems of Passion shortly after in May 1883.

The newlyweds lived for a short time in Robert's home town of Meriden, Connecticut, before moving to New York City and then to Granite Bay in the Short Beach area of Branford, Connecticut. They built two homes and several cottages on Long Island Sound where they would hold gatherings of their literary and artistic friends.

On May 27, 1887, Ella gave birth to a son. Tragically he was only to survive for a few short hours.

In the early years of their marriage, they both developed an interest in theosophy, New Thought, and spiritualism. As this developed Robert and

Ella Wheeler Wilcox promised each other that whoever died first would return and attempt to communicate with the other.

Ella had by now published many books of poetry as well as novels and other writings. Her writing life was filled with success on a national scale. Some volumes were collections based on a theme others on a particular time. Some of her war poetry that centred on the Great War in Europe is quite compelling. As she was never considered literary but rather mass market a lot of her work has not received the recognition that other lesser writers have obtained.

In 1916 after thirty years of marriage Robert Wilcox died. Ella was naturally devastated and desperate. Rather than dissipate her grief seemed to grow ever more intense as the days and weeks went by with no message from him. She journeyed to California to see the Rosicrucian astrologer, Max Heindel, seeking help in her sorrow as to why she had no word from Robert. She writes:

"In talking with Max Heindel, the leader of the Rosicrucian Philosophy in California, he made very clear to me the effect of intense grief. Mr. Heindel assured me that I would come in touch with the spirit of my husband when I learned to control my sorrow. I replied that it seemed strange to me that an omnipotent God could not send a flash of his light into a suffering soul to bring its conviction when most needed. Did you ever stand beside a clear pool of water, asked Mr. Heindel, and see the trees and skies repeated therein? And did you ever cast a stone into that pool and see it clouded and turmoiled, so it gave no reflection? Yet the skies and trees were waiting above to be reflected when the waters grew calm. So God and your husband's spirit wait to show themselves to you when the turbulence of sorrow is quieted".

It seemed good advice. She wrote herself a short affirmative prayer to help calm her inner turmoil and would repeat it to herself over and over:

"I am the living witness: The dead live: And they speak through us and to us: And I am the voice that gives this glorious truth to the suffering world: I am ready, God: I am ready, Christ: I am ready, Robert."

She had already written in 1915 a booklet 'What I Know About New Thought which had sold over 50,000 copies. These and other books on New Thought, together with her expanding efforts to educate a wider audience to the powers of positive thinking, were a great comfort to her.

Ella expresses this unique blend of New Thought, Spiritualism and Reincarnation with these powerful words:

"As we think, act, and live here today, we built the structures of our homes in spirit realms after we leave earth, and we build karma for future lives, thousands of years to come, on this earth or other planets. Life will assume new dignity, and labour new interest for us, when we come to the knowledge that death is but a continuation of life and labour, in higher planes".

Ella fell ill in France in early 1919. It was breast cancer. She was taken initially to England and then back to her home. She died of the cancer on October 31, 1919.

Her final words in her autobiography 'The Worlds and I' were:

"From this mighty storehouse (of God, and the hierarchies of Spiritual Beings) we may gather wisdom and knowledge, and receive light and power, as we pass through this preparatory room of earth, which is only one of the innumerable mansions in our Father's house. Think on these things".

A Concise Bibliography
1872   Drops of water, poems.
1873   Shells.
1876   Maurine.
1883   Poems of Passion.
1886   Mal Moule'e, a novel.
1886   Perdita, and other stories.
1888   The Adventures of Miss Volney.
1888   Poems of Pleasure.
1891   A Double Life.
1891   How Salvator Won, and other recitations.
1892   Was it Suicide?
1892   The Beautiful Land of Nod.
1892   An Erring Woman's Love.
1892   Sweet Danger.
1893   The Song of the Sandwich.
1893   Men, Women and Emotions.
1896   An Ambitious Man.
1896   Custer, and other poems.
1897   Three Women.
1897   Roger Merritt's Crime.
1901   Every-day Thoughts in Prose and Verse.
1901   Poems of Power.
1902   The Heart of the New Thought.
1902   Kingdom of Love and How Salvator Won.
1902   The Other Woman's Husband.
1902   Poems of Life.

1904	Around the Year with Ella Wheeler Wilcox.
1904	A Woman of the World.
1905	Mizpah; or, the story of Esther, poetical drama in four acts.
1905	Poems of Love.
1905	Poems of Reflection.
1905	The Story of a literary career.
1906	Poems of Sentiment.
1906	New Thought pastels.
1906	Poems of Peace.
1907	The Kingdom of love, and other poems.
1907	The Love Sonnets of Abelard and Heloise.
1908	New Thought - common sense and what life means to me.
1908	Poems of Cheer.
1908	Selected Poems.
1909	Poems of Progress and New Thought Pastels.
1909	Sailing Sunny Seas.
1910	Diary of a Faithless Husband.
1910	The New Hawaiian Girl; a play.
1910	Poems of Experience.
1910	Yesterdays.
1911	Are you Alive?
1912	Picked Poems.
1912	Gems from Ella Wheeler Wilcox.
1912	The Englishman and other Poems.
1914	Poems of Problems.
1914	The art of Being Alive.
1914	Cameos.
1914	Lest we Forget.
1914	Poems of Ella Wheeler Wilcox.
1915	Poems of Optimism.
1916	World Voices.
1916	More Poems.
1916	Poems of Purpose.
1917	Poetical Works of Ella Wheeler Wilcox.
1918	Sonnets of Sorrow and Triumph.
1918	The Worlds and I.
1919	Poems.
1919	Cinema Poems and others.
1919	Hello Boys!

Published Posthumously

1920	Poems of Affection.
1920	Great Thoughts For Each Day's Life.
1924	Collected Poems of Ella Wheeler Wilcox.
1927	Gems from E.W.Wilcox

www.ingramcontent.com/pod-product-compliance
Lightning Source LLC
Chambersburg PA
CBHW061255040426
42444CB00010B/2387